SINGAPORE A–Z

A PICTORIAL OVERVIEW

BENJAMIN YAP
with text by Vanessa Wan

Marshall Cavendish
Editions

Additional photos by: Goodwood Park Hotel: 48 (bottom), 49 (top right)

This edition published by Marshall Cavendish Editions
An imprint of Marshall Cavendish International
1 New Industrial Road, Singapore 536196

Other Marshall Cavendish Offices:
Marshall Cavendish Ltd. 119 Wardour Street, London W1F 0UW, UK • Marshall Cavendish Corporation.
99 White Plains Road, Tarrytown NY 10591-9001, USA • Marshall Cavendish International (Thailand) Co Ltd.
253 Asoke, 12th Flr, Sukhumvit 21 Road, Klongtoey Nua, Wattana, Bangkok 10110, Thailand • Marshall Cavendish
(Malaysia) Sdn Bhd, Times Subang, Lot 46, Subang Hi-Tech Industrial Park, Batu Tiga, 40000 Shah Alam,
Selangor Darul Ehsan, Malaysia

Marshall Cavendish is a trademark of Times Publishing Limited

National Library Board Singapore Cataloguing in Publication Data

Yap, Benjamin, 1972–
Singapore A-Z : a pictorial overview / Benjamin Yap ; with text by Vanessa Wan.
— Singapore : Marshall Cavendish Editions, 2006.
p. cm.
Previously published: Times Editions-Marshall Cavendish, c2004.
ISBN-13 : 978-981-232-807-6
ISBN-10 : 981-232-807-6

1. Singapore—Pictorial works. I. Wan, Vanessa. II. Title.

DS609.2
959.57 — dc21   SLS2006007803

Printed in Singapore by Times Graphics Pte Ltd

If you've visited Singapore
You'll know just what we mean
When we say the city is
So fresh and clean and green.

With lots to see and more to do
Plus delicious treats galore
Let us start to count the ways
How we are uniquely Singapore!

DEPARTURES

SCHEDULED TIME	NEW TIME	TO	FLIGHT	CHECK-IN ROWS	REMARKS	BOARDING
07:25	:	HONG KONG	Valuair VF902	13 -	LAST CALL	●
07:30	:	JAKARTA	GA823	14 -	LAST CALL	●
07:35	:	COLOMBO	UL316	10 -	LAST CALL	●
07:40	:	CHENGDU	CA434	07 -	LAST CALL	●
07:45	:	BANGKOK	TG422	03 -	LAST CALL	●
07:50	08:10	BANGALORE	IC958	10 -	GATE OPEN	
07:55	:	JAKARTA	Valuair VF202	13 -	LAST CALL	● 07 31
08:00		TOKYO-NARITA	JL712	11 -		●
08:00		TOKYO-NARITA	AA7214	11 -	BOARDING	●
08:05		HONG KONG	CX710	08 -	BOARDING	●
08:05		HONG KONG	AA6094	08 -	BOARDING	●
08:10		TAIPEI	CI662	12 -	GATE OPEN	
08:20		BANGKOK	TG402	03 -	LAST CALL	●
08:25		CHENNAI	IC556	09 -	GATE OPEN	
08:35		NANCHANG	CZ354	06 -	GATE OPEN	
08:40		KUNMING	MU464	02		
09:15		SYDNEY	QANTAS QF32	05		
09:15		SYDNEY	BA7372	05		
09:20		PERTH	QANTAS QF72	05		
09:20		PERTH	BA7376	05 -		

A is for the Airport at Changi
So modern and efficient
With food, shopping and entertainment
It's one of Singapore's many attractions.

The Singapore Changi Airport, one of the best airports in the world, can be found on the island's eastern tip. A free Skytrain shuttle runs at regular intervals between its two busy terminals. It takes about 30 minutes to get to Changi Airport from the city on the Mass Rapid Transit (MRT) train.

WHERE
Civil Aviation Authority of Singapore
Singapore Changi Airport
P.O. Box 1
Singapore 918141
Tel: (65) 6542 1122
www.changiairport.com.sg

B

A t the Botanic Gardens
A variety of plants and flowers thrive
In this splendid oasis
Of tropical natural life.

Located close to the heart of the city, the Botanic Gardens, with a picturesque lake for picnics, houses thousands of species of rare plant life. The gardens are also home to the National Orchid Garden — the largest orchid display in the world, featuring over 1,000 orchid species and 2,000 hybrids. *Au Jardin Les Amis,* arguably Singapore's best French restaurant, is also located in a restored colonial building within the gardens.

WHERE

1 Cluny Road, Singapore 259569

Tel: (65) 6471 7361

Fax: (65) 6473 7983

www.sbg.org.sg

Open from 5 am to 12 midnight daily

Free admission.

National Orchid Garden: 8:30 am to 7 pm daily. S$2 for adults, S$1 for children under 12 and senior citizens above 60.

C is for the courtyard a
Whose cloistered w
When nuns occupie
Saying prayers to G

Previously a convent, Chijmes now houses shopping outlets and restaurants. The grounds, located along Victoria Street, boasts five neo-gothic buildings, including the restored Caldwell House, built in 1840 by G.D. Coleman. This beautiful building once housed the convent's nuns and the sewing room of the Mother Superior. The sunken forecourt, waterfalls and fountains are especially romantic at night. Also noteworthy are the stained-glass windows of Chijmes Hall.

WHERE

30 Victoria Street, Singapore 187996

Tel: (65) 6338 2529

Fax: (65) 6334 3801

www.chijmes.com.sg

K

nowledge and thrills await the curious
At the Singapore Discovery Centre
With giant exhibits and 3D shows
To arouse your sense of wonder.

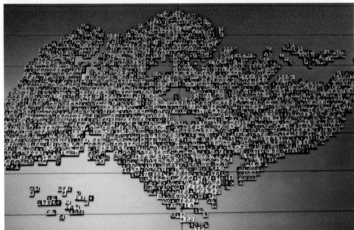

Discover Singapore through its defence and technological history. Explore a giant map — created from over 2,500 photographs of Singaporeans — and the IWERKS Theatre's 5-storey-high screen. You can also find a computer-simulated firing range using real weapons and Southeast Asia's largest motion simulator. Climb into actual jets, tanks and boats used by the Singapore military. Or if you prefer something more sedate, take a leisurely stroll around the centre's large lake.

WHERE

510 Upper Jurong Road, Singapore 638365

Tel: (65) 6792 6188

Fax: (65) 6792 1233

www.sdc.com.sg

Open from 9 am to 7 pm, Tue to Sun

D rama, the arts and culture
Can be found at the Esplanade
Below the iconic 'durians'
Music and dance take centrestage.

The uniquely designed Esplanade – Theatres on the Bay is Singapore's latest landmark and is situated on prime waterfront land by Marina Bay. Affectionately referred to as the 'durians' by locals, the Esplanade is Singapore's cultural icon. From jazz to pop to classical music, the Esplanade stages them all in its two main theatres and ancillary studios. Open-air performances enliven the Esplanade's waterfront promenade. There are also galleries showcasing contemporary art and a mall with a variety of food and retail outlets.

WHERE

1 Esplanade Drive, Singapore 038981

Tel: (65) 6828 8222

Fax: (65) 6337 3633

www.esplanade.com

The British defended Fort Canning
During the time of the Second World War
While the Fullerton is now a grand hotel
An icon of colonial Singapore.

Fort Canning was home to Malay rulers in the fourteenth century, and deceased royalty were believed to have been buried there. This includes the grave of Sultan Iskandar Shah, Singapore's last Malay ruler. Today, the hill is a popular venue for wedding photography, outdoor concerts and movie screenings. Tucked into the side of the hill is the Battle Box, the largest military operations complex in Singapore during World War II. Modern visitors can relive the morning of 15 February 1942, when Singapore fell to the Japanese invaders.

WHERE

51 Canning Rise, Singapore 179872

Tel: (65) 6332 1302

Fax: (65) 6339 9715

Built in 1928, the neoclassical Fullerton Building has housed the General Post Office, the Exchange, The Chamber of Commerce and the Inland Revenue Authority of Singapore in its time. Beautifully restored and reopened in 2001 as the Fullerton Hotel, this epitome of Palladian architecture in Singapore now plays host to eminent guests and is an ideal venue for fairy tale weddings.

WHERE
1 Fullerton Square, Singapore 049178
Tel: (65) 6733 8388
Fax: (65) 6735 8388
www.fullertonhotel.com

At the Goodwood Park Hotel
A national monument in grey and white
You'll find charming rooms and suites
And sumptuous durian delights.

Built in 1900 as the Teutonia Club for Germans, the stately Goodwood Park Hotel's historical heritage has been preserved by careful restoration work and modern touches. The king of fruits is also crowned at the Goodwood Park Hotel; the hotel's bakery is renowned for its delicious durian pastries.

WHERE

22 Scotts Road, Singapore 228221

Tel: (65) 6737 7411

Fax: (65) 6732 8558

www.goodwoodparkhotel.com

H
is for Holland Village
Whose pulse goes on through the night
Family-friendly by day, youthful by dusk
This Little Bohemia is quite a sight.

From fresh market produce to exquisite antiques, old-style coffee shops to hip dessert cafés, Holland Village is a place buzzing with youthful energy.

www.hollandvillage.com.sg

I is for the Istana

Home to our esteemed Head of State

Watch for the next public holiday

When the palace throws open its gates.

Istana means 'palace' in Malay. Previously known as Government House, the Istana was designed by J.F.A. McNair and built in 1869 using convict labour. It is the official residence of the President of the Republic of Singapore. Its grounds are open to the public on major public holidays.

WHERE
Orchard Road, Singapore 238823
www.istana.gov.sg

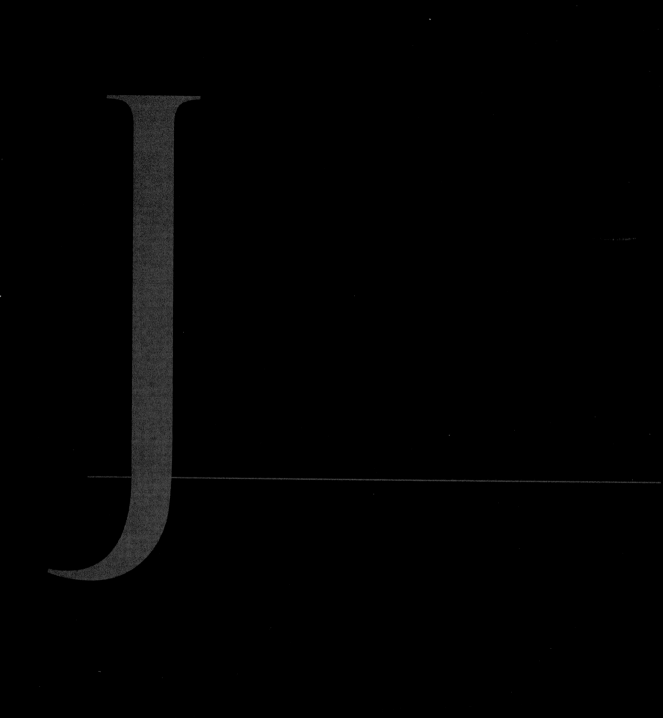

T alent awaits at the Jurong Bird Park
Home to our colourful feathered friends
With over 8,000 birds in a rainforest setting
Watch them flutter in song and dance.

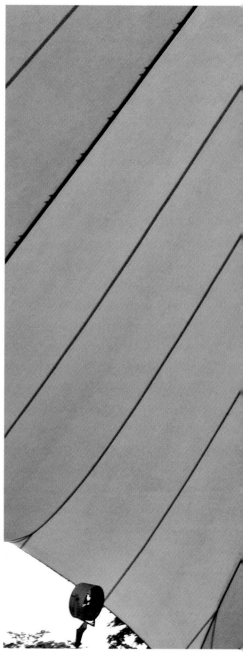

Housing nearly 600 species of birds, the Jurong Bird Park boasts the world's largest walk-in aviary as well as a simulated rainforest thunderstorm, held at noon each day. The lory loft is the world's largest lory flight aviary.

WHERE

2 Jurong Hill, Singapore 628925

Tel: (65) 6265 0022

Fax: (65) 6261 1869

www.birdpark.com.sg

Open from 8 am to 6 pm daily

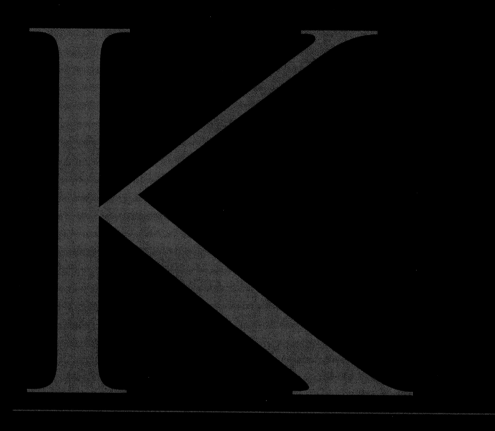

In Remembrance
of those who died in the
war in defence of
Singapore

from
DER Hillgove
& ashabook

T

he Kranji War Memorial
Salutes heroes from the past
Who fought bravely in World War II
And now rest in peace at last.

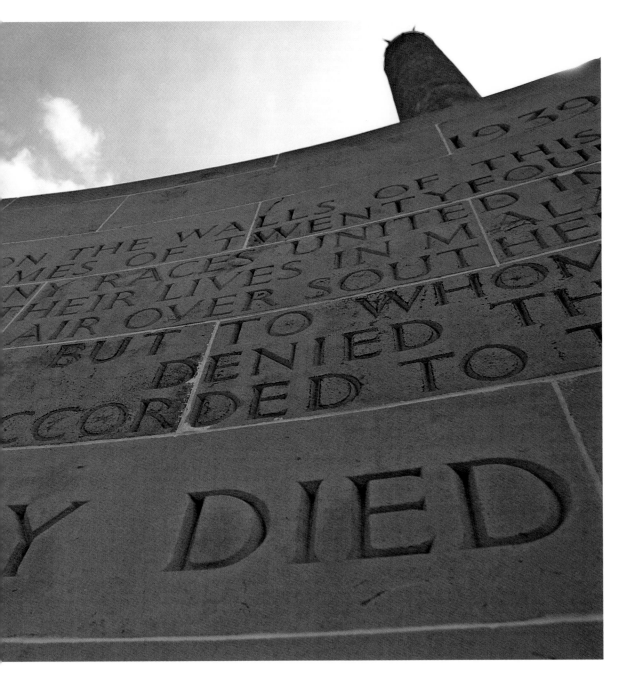

Built in memory of the Allied soldiers who fought and died in the defence of Singapore during World War II, the Kranji War Memorial is beautifully landscaped with walls bearing inscriptions of the heroes' names. Singapore's past presidents are also buried here.

WHERE

9 Woodlands Road, Singapore 738656

www.newasia-singapore.com

Open from 7 am to 6 pm daily

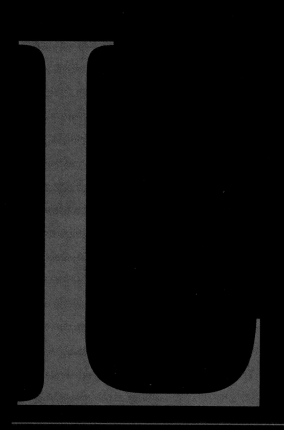

L is for Lau Pa Sat
The old Victorian market at Telok Ayer
Now a national monument, a food paradise
And a great supper spot for hot tea and satay.

SELF SERVICE

FATMAN SAT

MUTTON $0.50¢   **PRAWN** $

CHICKEN $0.50¢   **KETUPAT** $

BEEF $0.50¢   **STALL**

PERUT BABAT - 50¢

Lau Pa Sat is the largest remaining Victorian filigree cast-iron structure is Southeast Asia. Built in 1894, it began as a wet market and is now a popular food centre open late into the night. Especially popular are *satay* (grilled meat on skewers) enjoyed with a large glass of hot *teh tarik* (milk tea).

WHERE

18 Raffles Quay, Singapore 048582

M

is for the Merlion
Beast of ancient symbolism
Head of a lion and body of a fish
Majestic icon of Singapore's tourism.

The half-lion, half-fish Merlion sculpture has been Singapore's national icon since 15 September 1972. After all, the city's name is derived from the Sanskrit words "singa" and "pura" which together mean "lion city". The Merlion is located in an urban park overlooking Marina Bay.

N

is for the Night Safari
The world's first such zoo of its kind
Sly striped hyenas and shy horned rhinos
Are some of the animals you will find.

NIG

SAFA

SINGAPOR

Opened in 1994, the Night Safari is the first wildlife park designed to be viewed at night. With more than 1,000 nocturnal animals and 142 species, it offers an unrivalled opportunity to see the nocturnal happenings in a zoo after dark.

WHERE
80 Mandai Lake Road,
Singapore 729826
Tel: (65) 6269 3411
Fax: (65) 6367 2974
www.nightsafari.com.sg
Open from 7:30 pm to midnight

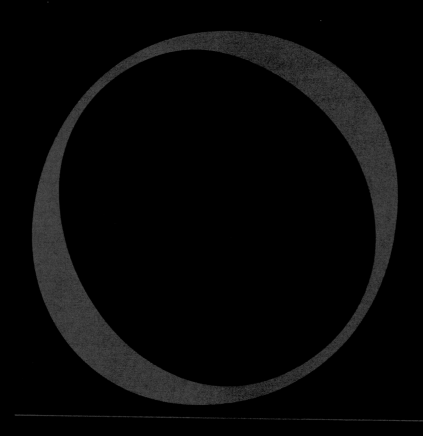

Orchard Road with its crowds and stores
Is a shopper's paradise
Especially during the Great Singapore Sale
Where everything is at its lowest price.

Orchard Road is Singapore's dynamic shopping district with bargains for everyone. Streets in the area were named after the many nutmeg plantations, pepper farms and fruit orchards that existed here in the 1840s, as well as their plantation owners like Oxley, Carnie (Cairnhill) and Cuppage. Every year, the Great Singapore Sale, held between May and July, gives Singaporeans and tourists ever more reason to shop.

M
ore than a large patch of grass
Is the Padang in front of City Hall
The Japanese surrender, soccer matches
National Day parades: the Padang has seen
them all.

The Padang, which means "field" in Malay, was where the colonial community gathered for their recreational activities in the past; from cricket to after-dinner strolls. The Padang was an important aspect of British colonial life. The Singapore Cricket Club still stands there today, and cricket is still played on weekends. The Padang has also witnessed momentous events in Singapore's history, such as the surrender of the Japanese to Lord Louis Mountbatten in 1945. Singapore held its first National Day parade at the Padang in 1966.

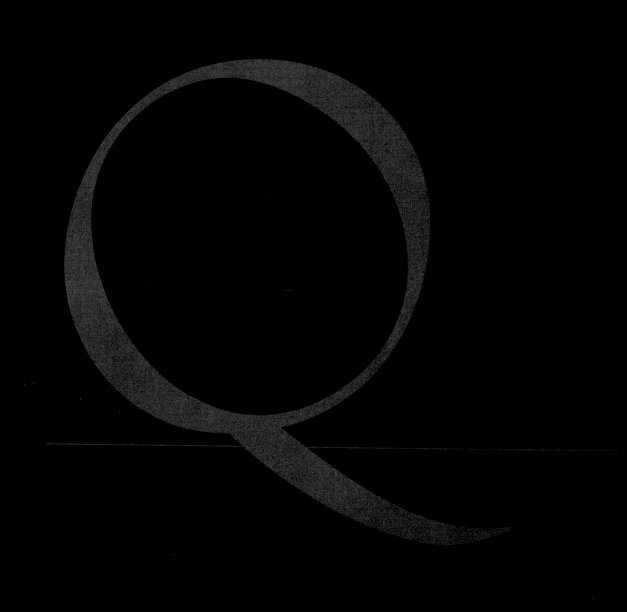

Boat Quay, Clarke Quay & Robertson Quay
A bustling stretch along the Singapore River
Once a commercial lifeline
Now a great place for drinks and dinner.

The three quays along the Singapore River host a myriad of eateries, bars, pubs, discos and night clubs. Have pre-dinner drinks at Clarke Quay before taking the bumboat to Boat Quay for dinner by the water. End the evening by bar hopping or dancing the night away in one of many nightclubs found at Robertson Quay.

R

is for the old Raffles Hotel
A charming grand old dame
Home of the famous Singapore Sling
Legend and lore is in its name.

Over a hundred years old and still a strong legend, this is widely considered to be one of the world's finest hotels. There are suites named after celebrities who once stayed there, including Charlie Chaplin, Somerset Maugham, Rudyard Kipling and Noel Coward.

WHERE

1 Beach Road, Singapore 189673

Tel: (65) 6337 1886

Fax: (65) 6339 7650

www.raffleshotel.com

The Sultan Mosque is a splendid sight
Its slender minarets rise up into the air
Underneath its large golden dome
Muslims raise their hands in prayer.

This national monument features the Saracenic style of architecture with domes and minarets. The original mosque on this site in North Bridge Road was named after Sultan Hussain Shah and built with a generous $3,000 grant from the East India Company.

WHERE
3 Muscat Street, Singapore 198833
Tel: (65) 6293 4405

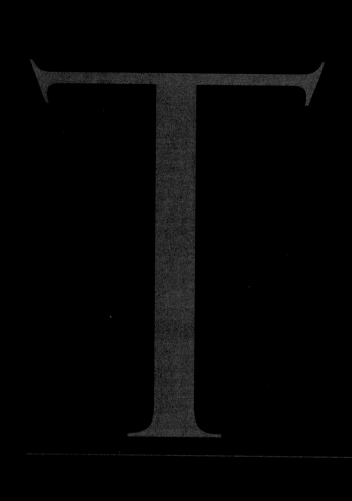

T

is for Thian Hock Keng Temple
Built by seamen in days of old
The devout still come to pray with joss-sticks
While some have their fortunes told.

Singapore's early forefathers were seamen who built this Chinese temple in 1821 in thanksgiving for their safe passage to Singapore. The temple was dedicated to the Goddess of Seafarers, Ma Zhu Po, and was sited on Singapore's original waterfront before land reclamation shifted it well inland. It is Singapore's oldest Chinese temple and is beautifully crafted using traditional joinery. Two fierce-looking door gods guard the temple's entrance.

WHERE

158 Telok Ayer Street, Singapore 048613

Tel: (65) 6423 4616

Fax: (65) 6423 4626

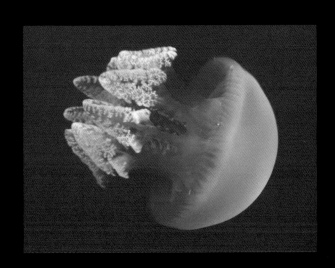

The fantastic Underwater World
Houses creatures beautiful and rare
Located on Sentosa, the isle getaway
Keeps the crowds returning there.

Fort Siloso
c. 1930s

Underwater World is Asia's largest tropical oceanarium, with a submerged walkway that offers breathtaking views of sharks, stingrays and moray eels. Sentosa was once a fishing village which later became a British military fort. Fort Siloso is one of the island's main attractions today. The Butterfly Park, Dolphin Lagoon, Musical Fountain show, virtual reality rides, beach bars, nature trails, and more make this the perfect island getaway for the weekend to soak up the sun and have fun. It is no wonder that Sentosa is considered Singapore's playground.

WHERE

Underwater World

80 Silosa Road, Singapore 098969

Tel: (65) 6275 0030

Fax: (65) 6275 0036

www.underwaterworld.com.sg

Open 9 am to 9 pm daily

www.sentosa.com.sg

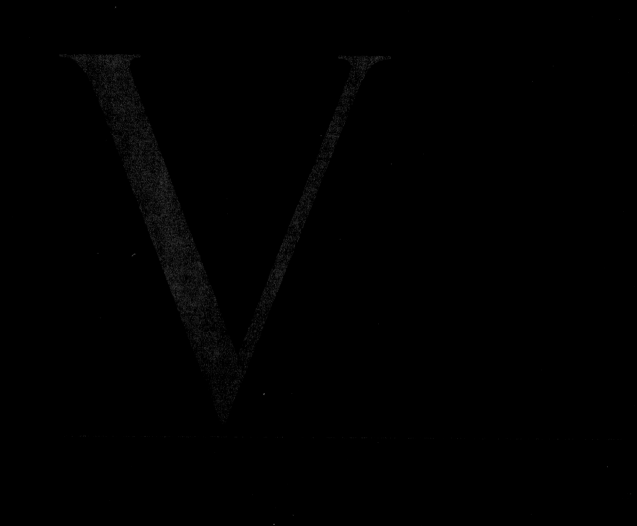

V
is for Victoria Theatre
And the Concert Hall next door
Symphonies have been playing
As Raffles watches Singapore.

The Victoria Theatre was built as Singapore's Town House in 1862, but it was not until 1905 that the Victoria Concert Hall opened next door. In front of the Concert Hall stands a bronze statue of Sir Stamford Raffles, which was moved to its present location from the Padang in 1919.

WHERE
9-11 Empress Place, Singapore 179556
www.sso.org.sg

W
is for water
So precious in old Chinatown
Drawn by bullock carts for immigrants
Who in every cramped space were found.

142

The first Chinese who arrived in Singapore endured harsh living conditions. The only sources of fresh water were found in Ann Siang Hill and Spring Street. Households collected water in bullock carts, thus giving rise to the local name for Chinatown — Niu Che Shui (Bullock Cart Water). Chinatown today is home to the new Chinatown Heritage Centre, which gives a glimpse into the life of the early Chinese immigrants and the tight and often squalid living conditions they had to endure. Chinatown is also home to the oldest and most important Hindu temple in Singapore: the Sri Mariamman Temple. This example of the juxtaposition of cultural symbols reflects the country's racial diversity.

WHERE

48 Pagoda St, Singapore 059207
Tel: (65) 6325 2878
Fax: (65) 6325 2879
www.chinatownheritage.com.sg
Open from 10 am to 7 pm daily

X marks the spot at Bukit Chandu
Where Malay Regiment soldiers fought well
Vastly outnumbered by the Japanese
Choosing death over dishonour, they fell.

of the swamps and
or tin and to plant
developed a well-
ds, railways and

"...I can't help feeling that the
security of the Fortress might
be better served by having a
stronger force in being outside
it... I consequently feel that the
answers to the possible threat
(of Japanese landing and
establishing an advanced base
on the mainland) is primarily
to be found in suitable mobile
forces in being in the Malay
Peninsula..."

*Major General William
Dobbie's letter
to War Office, 17th March
1936*

Japan's interest in
Malaya was known,
but British defence
planners assumed that

around Betet, if not
obstruct, any overland
invasion.

Major-General
Dobbie was fully
convinced that to
defend Singapore,
Britain must first
defend the whole of
Malaya.

193

uring this period, Japan
vas invading China, and in
need of vital commodities
nd tin for

e island of
The threat of
son of Malaya and
was finally seen as
inevitable

Soldiers built up the beach defence
with wire entanglements. Minefields
and big barriers to make amphibious
operations difficult.

To the British Overseas
Defence Committee, it
seemed clear that an attack
could come from the sea
and, or from Johore. The
therefore evolved a strategy
that took these alternatives
into account.

defence of Singapore
consisted of a series of
Guns Batteries. Contrary
to popular belief, some of
these guns were made
to fire both landward
and seaward.

FORT SILOSO
Fort Siloso guarded the western
entrance to Keppel
Harbour. By 1939, there were
two 6-inch MKs guns and two
rapid firing 12 pounder guns.

From the 1920s, Japan had
begun to emerge as a
serious threat to British
outposts in the Far East.
With drastic cuts in her
defence budget after World
War I, the British could no
longer maintain a strong
permanent naval defence
in the area. It therefore
decided to implement the
"Main Fleet to Singapore"
strategy, to defend not only
Singapore, but the rest of
her empire in the Far East,
and Australasia.

Many years prior to their
attack on Malaya in
December 1941, Japanese
military planners had studied
the Malayan terrain and
weighed harbour strategy, the
strategy and equipment needed
for the coming campaign.
Their immediate objective
and Capture of Singapore.

DECEMBER
8 1941

The highly trained and
battle hardened 25th Army
led by the Imperial General
Yamashita and elite troops
of the 5th Division, were
ordered to carry out the
Japanese offensive down
the Malaya peninsula and
capture Singapore, before
the Allies could deploy
their resources.

Certain that the
would first
from the sea,
th defence
planners were
confident that the
Main F
reinforcements
acr
wel
be

More than 1,400 soldiers of the Malay Regiment made their stand against 13,000 Japanese troops at Bukit Chandu (Opium Hill) in 1942 during World War II. The interpretive centre is a memorial to these brave heroes who paid the price for peace.

WHERE

31-K Pepys Road, Singapore 118458

Tel: (65) 6338 7978

Fax: (65) 6339 3583

www.s1942.org.sg

Open from 9 am to 5 pm, Tue to Sun

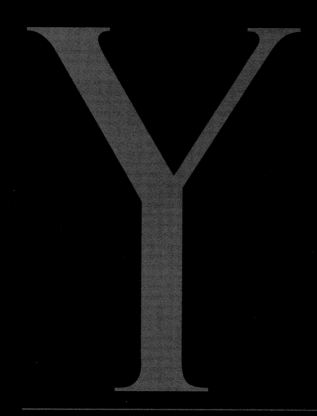

D
iscover a side of Singapore
Many tourists hardly see
Take the MRT to Yishun
And like a local be.

Explore Singapore from the comfort of the Mass Rapid Transit (MRT) train, and get off at the Yishun station to experience one of Singapore's heartlands. Next to the Yishun MRT station is the Northpoint Shopping Mall and cinemas. Take a walk through the blocks of flats and sneak a peek at how most Singaporeans live.

M
arvel at lions, tigers and apes
At the world-famous Singapore Zoo
Hop onto a tram or walk the trails
There's so much you can see and do.

Built in the early 1970s, this world-class zoo features more than 2,000 animals of nearly 250 species. An award-winning "open concept" zoo, the animals are kept in spacious, landscaped enclosures, separated from the visitors by concealed moats. See the regal white tigers or take an elephant ride. Curious monkeys come up close to play or people-watch.

WHERE

80 Mandai Lake Road, Singapore 729826

Tel: (65) 6269 3411

Fax: (65) 6367 2974

www.zoo.com.sg

Open from 8:30 am to 6 pm daily

Friendly folks, exotic food
A melting pot and more
Rich in heritage, sights and sounds
So uniquely Singapore.

So many great adventures
And there's still more in store
But for now, fond farewell, come again
With love from
Singapore!

Index

Recommended Websites on Singapore

http://www.visitsingapore.com

http://www.sg